ON THE MOVE

A Handbook
for
Exploring Creative Movement
with
Young Children

ON THE MOVE

A Handbook

for

Exploring Creative Movement

with

Young Children

by

Ginger Zukowski and Ardie Dickson

Southern Illinois University Press

Carbondale and Edwardsville

ROBERT MANNING
STROZIE LIBRARY

JUN 25 1990

Tallahassee, Florida

GV
452
Z85
1990

Copyright © 1990 by the Board of Trustees,
Southern Illinois University
All rights reserved
Printed in the United States of America
Edited and designed by Natalie S. Ihle
Production supervised by Natalia Nadraga
93 92 91 90   4 3 2 1

Library of Congress Cataloging-in-Publication Data

Zukowski, Ginger, 1951–
  On the move : a handbook for exploring creative movement with
young children / by Ginger Zukowski and Ardie Dickson.
      p. cm.
    Bibliography: p.
    1. Movement education.   2. Movement education—Study and teaching.
3. Early childhood education.   I. Dickson, Ardie.   II. Title.
GV452.Z85   1990
372'.216—dc19   88-37032
ISBN 0-8093-1542-4   CIP

The paper used in this publication meets the minimum requirements of
American National Standard for Information Sciences—Permanence
of Paper for Printed Library Materials, ANSI Z39.48-1984. ∞

To Gary Zukowski and Steve Dickson

Contents

Preface

This book is a practical how-to guide for integrating creative movement into the curriculum of young children. It is intended not only for child-care providers, but also for classroom teachers, dance and gym teachers, therapists, students in childhood education courses, and anyone wanting to integrate creative movement into the experiences of young children. One of the book's goals is to dispel the notion that teachers need extensive background in movement or dance to provide creative movement experiences for children. Knowing what is developmentally appropriate, understanding the elements of movement and dance, and having an open imagination are more important than professional dance technique. This book about movement and dance emphasizes the partnership between the children and the teacher.

The book delineates the importance of creative movement for children's motor, conceptual, social, and emotional development, and it provides guidelines for preparing to teach creative movement and suggestions for teachers. The book explains movement games and activities, which are accompanied by descriptions and directions, and the functions they serve in young children's development. The book also includes a sample session, as well as several activities that may be used to conclude a movement session. Another important feature of the book, a chapter on children with special needs, discusses sensory integration, physical handicaps, and the reality of mainstreaming children with disabilities. Since the book may be used as a primary text or as a supplementary text in college courses or workshops, assignments for each chapter are included at the back of the book. And the bibliography furnishes sources for further reading. In addition, the book has photographs, which enhance the already helpful text.

As you read *On the Move*, you will find that creative movement embraces such areas as music, language, drama, literature, and even math and science. And you will realize that creative movement is a part of both children and adults.

Sincere thanks to Lois Hickman, an occupational therapist; to Steve Paxton whose teaching of dance improvisation provided the basis for the ideas in this text; to the children of New Horizons, past and present; and to the children of Community Schools' dance classes in Boulder, Colorado.

Grateful acknowledgment is made to Matt Angiono for his poem "M-O-P," to Lois LaFond and her daughter Arisa for the use of the song "Rainbows," to Joe Hayes for the use of his story "Sky-Pushing Poles," and to Alfred A. Knopf, Inc. for permission to use the excerpt from Frederick Leboyer's *Loving Hands*.

And special thanks to Nancy Bizzarro for her photos.

ON THE MOVE

1

The Importance of Creative Movement

"As long as there is life, there is movement, and to move is hence to satisfy a basic and eternal need."[1] There is unique power in dance as a way of learning and communicating because movement is humankind's oldest and most basic means of expression. The first things we do are to move and to grow.

Life was so rich within the womb!
Rich in noises and sounds. Both from the mother's body and from the outside world.
But mostly there was movement.
Continuous movement.
When the mother sits, stands, walks, turns—movement, movement, movement. . . .
All pleasant, comforting sensations for the small creature inside.
And when the mother is quiet, either sitting or lying down, even when she goes to sleep, her steady, sure breathing keeps on, rocking the little traveler inside her, gently, continuously.
All day and all night, the endless flow of sensations and movements.
But now . . . ![2]

Movement and touch are the first sources of play and learning

1. Ted Shawn, *Dance We Must* (New York: Haskell House Publishing, 1974), 1.
2. Frederick Leboyer, *Loving Hands* (New York: Alfred A. Knopf, 1976), 9.

that adults provide to infants (rocking, patting, stroking, swaying, bouncing) and that infants themselves investigate (kicking, reaching, smiling, wiggling, tilting their heads).[3] Infants move to learn. As toddlers and older children grow, they learn to move with greater skill. Our role as teachers is to encourage children to discover and to extend this impulse to move. And as we help young children extend movement possibilities and add new skills, we foster self-expression and problem solving. "Movement experiences shape the order and meaning that children ascribe to their world, furnishing . . . the building blocks of their development."[4]

Creative movement truly promotes healthy growth in all areas of young children's development: motor, conceptual, social, and emotional. Creative movement allows children to improve their motor skills, to become aware of their bodies as a whole, and to isolate body parts. Children learn about their bodies in relation to space, and they become skillful in controlling the starting, the stopping, the speed, and the direction of movement. An obvious benefit of creative movement is full body involvement in a vigorous and enjoyable activity. Creative movement also enables children to grow conceptually, to put their own ideas into movement, to use problem-solving skills, and to think of new ways to use their bodies. Children can use concrete movements to describe their feelings, a character in a story, or an element of nature. Through concrete actions, such as isolating movements, moving with a partner, skipping in a certain pathway, or choosing a new way to hop, children touch on such abstract concepts as spatial awareness, self-control, and acceptance of others' ideas. All children can use movement to communicate, and those children delayed in verbal skills will especially benefit from this outlet. Also, movement can help children develop an aesthetic awareness of the beauty of their own bodies as well as those of others. Creative movement activities further aid in social development for they provide a good way for

3. Joanne F. Oppenheim, *Kids and Play* (New York: Ballantine Books, 1984), 1–37.

4. Cynthia Berrol, "The Effects of Two Movement Therapy Approaches," *American Journal of Dance Therapy* 7 (1984): 33.

children to be with other children in an atmosphere of cooperation and shared endeavor. Such activities present the uniqueness of each child in a noncompetitive way. These activities can also be used to develop behavior that helps children to be successful and comfortable in a group. Creative movement can help children to grow emotionally—it helps children feel successful and appreciated because there is no right or wrong way to move. Children can act out feelings in a safe atmosphere. They can express controlled aggressive feelings, as well as fear and happiness. And children who are less physically assertive in other situations, such as climbing or tricycle riding, can release their feelings through creative movement in a less threatening environment.

Creative movement also nourishes kinesthesia, the sense of how to move. The kinesthetic sense dictates the perception of where and how to place your foot when stepping off a ladder. As you hold a cup of coffee while you are reading, you can sense where to replace the cup and with what speed, as well as the correct force to apply. As you set the cup down, you do not need sight; you rely on your kinesthetic sense. Creative movement can extend this important sense. And as the children in your group become more experienced in moving around each other in the same space, they will do much less bumping and little falling. Useful suggestions, such as "Move to the empty spaces," "Try to hear and see all around your body as you go," and "Find your stillness when the music stops," will help the group move well together.

Spatial awareness is an integral part of creative movement sessions. The position in space is important, as when forming a circle for warm-ups at the beginning of a session. The body's relationship to objects and persons outside the self becomes a factor as dancers move through space together without bumping. Spatial awareness invokes as many senses as possible. And, with practice, spatial relationships (between, among, around, next to) can be visually and kinesthetically developed. Personal space can be explained using the image of a large transparent balloon around each of the children's bodies. Suggest that the balloons be blown up to be a bit bigger than their bodies and that the balloons do not bump. Children

Creative Movement Develops a Child's Sense of How to Move

carry this personal space as they move around the room without touching anyone or anything. To prevent children from touching someone in their paths, advise them to stop (put on the brakes), dodge (move quickly to one side or the other), slow down (back up), use their eyes (to go around), and use their ears (to hear another's footsteps).

When children use their bodies, minds, and imaginations in their movement activities and dance improvisations, or when they see others' improvisations, they have an aesthetic experience. Such a response feels good and leads them to find beauty in themselves and ultimately in their environment. For instance, a child asked to make an angry movement and an angry sound knows when just the right solution has been found, and so does the audience. Their faces seem to say, "That worked." In creative movement and dance, children are free to reveal their uniqueness. Observations such as "Josh's shape is very wide and strong," "That's a movement I've never seen before," and "Kate and Sarah have made a long tunnel

*Creative Movement Enhances a
Child's Self-Image*

shape" help the children feel competent and successful without
singling out anyone as better. You have asked the children to apply
their whole being to a problem and to arrive at a solution, so they
naturally will be pleased with the results. You will begin to see
each child's self-image emerge and in many cases improve as you
work together.

Imagery stimulates the whole child (the body, the mind, and
the imagination) and is the starter or catalyst for creative movement, but movement itself is the content of dance. Describing the
shape, size, direction, and speed of a visual image such as a lion, a
baseball pitcher, a marionette, or a spider web leads to expressive
movement.[5] Ask a child to dance like a lion, and you will get a lot
of crawling and growling. It is not that the child is pretending to be
a lion. We are people with two legs and fingers. Thus, to get the

5. Alma M. Hawkins, *Creating Through Dance* (Englewood Cliffs, N.J.:
Prentice-Hall, 1964), 5.

essence of a lion, the child must ask questions. What shape is a lion, wide or narrow? What direction will the lion move? How fast will the lion go? You may ask the children to show you the lion's strong, soft, back paws. By asking the children to play with the space, timing, direction, and force of their movements, they will discover that the content of their dances has variety and expression and that the movements are within their control. Thus, their movement repertoires will expand. The use of imagery to develop and stimulate a rich movement repertoire is essential. And this approach attempts to capture the essence of a visual or auditory image through fresh and imaginative movement.

With varieties of activities and acceptable solutions, the children lose much of their self-consciousness and progress to new levels of learning and communicating through movement. The progress becomes evident as the children grow in their feelings of confidence and positive self-image and are able to move on to more complicated concepts and activities. This book provides skill-development movement activities, both locomotor (traveling) and axial (stationary), as well as structured dance improvisations (improvisation machines) designed to promote children's overall development.

2

Preparation and Suggestions for Teachers

You do not need professional dance training to teach creative movement. You need only understand that movement is the content of dance and that all bodily movement exists in space and time and is done with a certain energy flow or dynamic quality. Take some time to experience these elements of movement, and realize that they are present with infinite variations in every dance and, indeed, in all movement. Everyday movements include each element. Movement activities (chapter 3) and improvisation machines (chapter 4) focus primarily on one dance element and on one or two specific tools within that element. Focusing on one specific element of dance for each activity provides an objective. In the following list, the respective tools follow each dance element.

Body. Creative movement promotes internal awareness of the body. A movement can involve the *total body* or *isolated body parts.* Movement may be done by leading with one side of the body or by alternating the right and left sides of the body. It is important for children to experience movement that crosses the midline, or the center of the body, and to try movements such as hops and turns in both directions.

Space. Creative movement promotes awareness of the body in space as it relates to external objects. The space element refers to the size, shape, focus, direction, and level of movement. The *size* of a particular movement can be small, medium, large, or larger than the body (which involves a partner). Body *shape* can be described as symmetrical (the same on each side) or asymmetrical (different on each side). The direction of the face, eyes, and sternum determines the *focus* of a movement. A collapsing or a downward movement can have an upward focus. Locomotor movements travel in various *directions:* forwards, backwards, sidewards, on the diagonal (a forty-five-degree angle from the front of the body), and on the diagonal of the room (the longest straight line in the room). Body shape and locomotor movements have various *levels:* low level (on the floor or sitting), middle level (squatting or bending or kneeling), high level (standing or stretching), and elevation (off the floor).

Time. Creative movement improves motor planning, which is the brain's ability to conceive, organize, and carry out a sequence of unfamiliar actions, and creative movement improves children's rhythmic responses. Movement occurs in a particular time as does music, sometimes with *rhythm* patterns or beats, always with a certain length or *duration*, and with a slow, moderate, or fast *tempo.* Rhythm patterns can be added to any movement for variation. Duration can be extended or shortened. And tempo can be accelerated or decelerated with control.

Quality. The quality of a movement is expressive. The force (heavy, light, pushing, or pulling) applied to a movement gives the movement intensity. A *sustained* movement quality is smooth and flowing with no stops. A *swinging* quality has a pendular movement with a drop-lift-drop-lift effect that forms a swinging arc that circumscribes the bottom of a circle in space. A movement with a sudden release of energy and a sudden stop, or a move and stop effect, has a *percussive* quality. A *suspended* movement quality has a momentary pause before gravity pulls the body toward the floor. A balance and a swing have moments of suspension. A rapid succession of percussive movements has a *vibratory* or shaking quality. Another movement quality, a *collapse,* or a fall with no resulting noise, is a complete rendering of weight to gravity, which retains just enough muscle tension to make a soft landing.

8

The four dance elements are analyzed in the following example, which uses the image of ice. Children asked to move across the room as if it were full of ice will express this image with their movements. The children may slide quickly around the floor in tight, closed, bent shapes, then fall to the floor with no noise, and vibrate their arms. This movement solution is listed below in the first column, and the corresponding dance elements are listed in the second column followed by the specific tools in parentheses.

Slide	Time (rhythm—slide in 2/4 time)
Quickly	Time (tempo)
Around and around	Space (direction)
Tight, closed, bent shape	Space (size, shape, middle level)
Fall with no noise	Quality (collapse)
Vibrate arms	Quality (vibratory movement)
	Body (isolation of the arms)

The general elements of dance and many specific tools are integrated into these movements. When designing movement activities, however, you should focus on only one or two elements of dance.

As you work with children and dance, you develop the eye of a collector. Begin to look at your favorite books, records, poems, and songs as movement starters.

Check your own record collection and the collections of friends, the library, and garage sales before going to the record store. All categories of music are possibilities, so set aside several kinds of music. Try music children may not have heard before. Musical collages are also interesting, and they add variety to accompaniments. The following musical selections may be used to make tape collages to accompany the movement activities and improvisation machines in chapters 3 and 4.

For jazz sounds, try Cal Tjader, Grover Washington, Miles Davis, Lionel Hampton, and John Coltrane. Try Pete Seeger, Woody

Guthrie, Kathy Fink, and Peter, Paul, and Mary for folk. Sound effect categories include electronics, transportation, weather ambience, and crowd and factory noises. For folk dance music, remember hammer dulcimer music, American bluegrass music, and music from various countries, which may include Russian, Greek, Peruvian, Irish, and African music. Chopin, Tchaikovsky, Satie, Debussy, and Aaron Copland are classical music favorites. And for Windham Hill recordings, try Andy Norel, Liz Story, and George Winston.

You may use poems and nursery rhymes either for their movement imagery or purely for their rhythm. You may use children as the source of poems, songs, and stories, or you may turn to your favorite children's literature. Children created the following poem and song, and Joe Hayes, a storyteller, contributed the "Sky-Pushing Poles" story.

> M-O-P starts to eat some cake.
> 1-2-3 goes up the tree.
> The rain comes falling down, down.
> The thunder and lightning hits those trees out there.
> Up goes the rain.
> Then it comes down again.
> The blue sky comes again.
> M-O-P.
>
> ("M-O-P" by Matt Angiono, age 3)

> Rainbow come out!
> Rainbow come out!
> With the sun
> And the trees
> With the birds
> And the bees
> Rainbow come out
> Come out for me![6]
>
> (Excerpt from "Rainbows" by Arisa LaFond, age 5)

6. Arisa LaFond, "Rainbows," *I Am Who I Am* (Boulder, Colo.: Boulder Children's Productions, 1985), Sound cassette.

A long time ago, when the creator made the world, he made a mistake. The sky was just above the people's heads, and they kept bumping their heads. It got to be so bad that the people in the village went to the wise people of the village. They said, "Wise people, what on earth are we going to do? We keep bumping our heads on the sky, and it's starting to get annoying." The wise people said, "Well, go to the swamp and cut yourselves sky-pushing poles."

So they went to the swamp and "whish" they cut their sky-pushing poles. When all the people got their sky-pushing poles, the wise people said, "Go," and the people said, "Yaa-ho!" and pushed the sky up.

They pushed the sky up pretty far. They could move around a bit more, but when they got up in the morning, they couldn't quite stretch enough. So the people in the village went to the wise people again, and the wise people said, "Go cut bigger sky-pushing poles." So the people went to the swamp again and "whish" they cut new sky-pushing poles. They made sure the new sky-pushing poles were a bit bigger than the first ones. When the wise people said, "Go," the people said, "Yaa-ho!" and pushed the sky up still higher. This time the sky was just about right. The people could stretch in the morning, and they could throw balls to play catch, but you know what? It was still pretty noisy because all the people on the other side of the the sky had parties all the time and the like.

So again the people went to the wise people, and the wise people said to them, "Get bigger sky-pushing poles." So they went to the swamp again and "whish" they cut b-i-i-g-g-g sky-pushing poles. When the wise people said, "Go," the people said, "Yaa-ho!" And, my goodness, they pushed the sky so hard that it flew off its hinges and went way up there where it is today.

Late at night you can see the light from the people on the other side of the sky shining through the little holes in the sky. And some people say that if you count every one of the holes you will know how many people said, "Yaa-ho!" and punched holes in the sky with their sky-pushing poles.

When moving to poems, songs, and stories, ask the children

to focus on qualities such as sustained or percussive movements. Use these movement qualities as they fit with the images in the poems, songs, and stories.

Add simple shapes and gestures to the song "Rainbows." When this becomes comfortable, you may broaden the arm gestures to include the whole body, and you may add ribbon props to extend the shapes. The shapes may be done on various levels, and a turn may be added for a change in direction.

In "Sky-Pushing Poles," sustained movements may be used for getting up in the morning and for walking to the swamp, and percussive movements may be used for pushing the sky and for chopping the poles. It will be a challenge for you and the children to add as much movement to "Sky-Pushing Poles" as possible as you push the sky, travel to and from the swamp, bump your heads, chop the poles, and more.

Certain well-selected props offer instant ideas for improvisation. How many ways can a scarf, ribbon, beanbag, or a length of elastic move? Floating, wiggling, swirling, balancing, and tossing motions are a few natural responses. Hoops may suggest an around and through game, and dress-up hats may lead to a character piece. Try a cape or a full skirt for a prop study with fabric as the inspiration. A prop supply may include hats, capes, hoops, ribbons, elastic, beanbags, foam balls, dot stickers, exercise mats, percussion instruments, colored flashlights, large fabric pieces, stretch fabric tubes, and a light behind a sheet for shadow dancing.

Kids are always in motion, on the playground, in the playroom, even in your lap. They use functional movements and expressive ones interchangeably and naturally. They use gravity when rolling down hills or swinging on a rope, and they overcome gravity when leaping over puddles or jumping for joy. Often children use body movements, more than language, to express their joy, discomfort, confusion, frustration, and excitement.

This book is meant as a springboard for activities and dance improvisations. Examples are given as a starting point for you and the children. Vary and adapt these ideas, and invent your own

Elastic as a Prop

versions. Be alert to suggestions of imagery and movement motifs that will come from the children and the surroundings.

You may base a problem-solving improvisation on a simple swinging movement that started on the playground earlier that day. For an accompaniment, find music that suggests swinging movements. How about the king of swing, Benny Goodman? Suggested instructions for the children are given below. The dance element and specific tools applicable are given parenthetically for some of the instructions.

"Let the music help you swing your arms." (Time—rhythm and tempo)

"Let the swing move to your head and neck; now add your whole torso." (Body—isolated body parts and total body)

"Can anyone make that swing travel?" (Space—direction.

13

Point out interesting direction changes and traveling steps you observe.)

"Can anyone swing faster than the music?" (Time—tempo. Beat your drum in a double-time rhythm.)

"Let a friend help you make a new swing that is bigger than your own body." (Space—size and shape)

"Swing in a way that I have never seen before." (Divide the class in half. Let one group watch while the other invents new swings. Then challenge the second group to make their own swings.)

"Try making your swings join together smoothly with no stops in between."

"Now we are ready to make a swinging dance. Begin in a still shape, and when you hear the music, do as many different swings as you can. When the music stops, show me your ending shape."

The children at New Horizons Preschool invented the following story, which was extended into a movement interpretation at group time later that morning. At the beginning of the school day, a garter snake was found and was the center of attention and observation for many children.

Once there was a snake. His name was Charlie. He was trying to get out of the oval tub. All the guys were looking at him. Ben and Jetley were petting him. He sticks out his tongue and goes *sssssssss*. He was in the water trying to get out. What do you think he eats? Bugs, bugs. Could he make an S shape? Yes. His tail is in the water. His tongue is sticking out. He's mad. You can tell he wants to eat bugs.

You, too, can start movement improvisations with ideas that come from the children or the environment. With the elements of dance in mind, expand the ideas, give them form, and add inspiring music to make spontaneous dances. For instance, a Roman shade may inspire a rolling dance. Venetian blinds may prompt open and closed shapes that rise and sink or jump up and down. And a clothes dryer may inspire a spinning and tumbling piece. The scenario for each of these ideas is similar to the ad-libbed swinging piece just described. Your words will guide the children through the dance experience.

A rope pulley attached to a bucket, which the children were using at playtime, inspired another ad-libbed dance. Pulling, rising, falling, rolling, and hand-over-hand movements were the natural responses to the pulley image. Playing with directions and levels provided the variations. The children were asked to select percussion instruments that they thought would go with the movements they had invented. Each child then chose either to dance or to play music, and the pulley piece was shown with the musical accompaniment.

Similarly, an improvisation can be based on music. Choose music that suggests traveling steps, preferably with tempo changes. Play the traveling music and ask the group to do all the traveling steps they can think of. Suggest that they invent traveling steps they have never done before. Say, "When you have invented three new traveling steps, please sit down in an empty space so I know you are ready." Have each half of the group show their new traveling steps at least three times. Say, "Now it is time to perform as many traveling steps as you can remember from those you did and from those you saw your friends do." The children may prefer to show their traveling steps as solos, duets, or trios. Challenge the children to include as many traveling steps as they possibly can remember and to stop in interesting ending shapes.

Creative movement can be done anywhere. Children have done beautiful hand dances accompanied by the car radio, buckled up in the backseat. Adapt the examples in this book to the available space by varying group size. Locomotor games can be played by taking turns in small groups in a very limited space. Pairs or trios can dance together, or half the class can move while the other half plays instruments. Any improvisation machine (chapter 4) can be performed in pairs in the center of a circle while the rest of the group sways or claps to the music. Our group calls this theater-in-the-round. The children can help move chairs and tables out of the way to create a stage area.

Dancing at School

A large space, such as a gymnasium or auditorium, gives the entire group a chance to move together. Locomotor movements can travel in long pathways, and when you say "Take some space" or "Find your own space," there is plenty of space to go around. It is worth the time and effort to plan an occasional field trip to a rented dance studio or gymnasium in the community. The games and improvisations that you have had fun with in the school take on a whole new feeling of expansion when arms can stretch their longest and legs can jump their highest. It is also interesting to play the locomotor games described in chapter 3 in a large space so that everyone can join in, and it is easier to avoid bumping into one another when galloping to the empty spaces, even if you add an arm-circling movement. When you call "Stick together," the natural response in the larger space may be huge group sculptures. Be sure to arrange for a sound system that will fill the space adequately.

If the large space is new to the children, expect them to want to run or gallop freely for the first few minutes. Having some lively

16

Dancing Outside

ragtime or jazz music playing as they arrive sets the tempo for this running around time. You can stop the music and the action at the same time. In a soft voice, ask the children to put their hands over their hearts. Then ask, "Is your heart beating faster or slower than when you arrived?" You may hear in response, "Faster, mine's faster." Say, "Good! That means you are working hard and your muscles are warming up." The group will then relax and be ready to form a circle for warm-ups.

The outdoors may give you a chance to move in a large space. Find a soft grassy area. Then you and the children can rope off a stage with tent stakes and twine. The defined space centers the children's concentration and will keep the group off the slide and merry-go-round. Although the outdoors can be distracting with traffic noises and bystanders, it offers free props such as shadows for partner dances, wind to move ribbons, or sand for making foot-prints as the children gallop or take giant steps.

A supportive climate, coupled with flexibility, will set the

17

tone. You already have a rapport with the children. They know your style, your humor, and they trust you. You know how to use the children's natural interests in your teaching methods. It is important to come to a creative movement session prepared with music, props, appropriate space, and movement ideas, but it is also essential to be flexible with your lesson plan. When something is working, be ready to extend, repeat, or vary that activity, even if you must leave out another planned activity. Conversely, some days are just "off." Either the group is not ready to concentrate or perhaps they are distracted by something that happened earlier that day. A flexible, intuitive teacher will respond by changing at the right moment to a quieter movement game or to a more vigorous one, or by extending or by shortening a particular movement activity.

Attention span grows with time, so each session's length can be gradually increased. You may start with one activity lasting maybe five or ten minutes for preschool groups and then work up to a full session, which includes a warm-up or isolation activity, a locomotor or axial movement game, an improvisation machine, and an ending. The entire session could last twenty minutes in a small space or extend forty-five minutes to an hour in a dance studio or an auditorium.

We hesitate to recommend a formal performance setting for children under the age of seven or eight. A formal performance puts undue pressure on them to remember the dance and to do it right, and it puts too much importance on the product. In any art form for young children, the process is much more important than the product.

At the same time, dance is a performing art that can be shared with an audience under carefully planned circumstances. If you and the children have a favorite dance improvisation that has been done many times in class for each other in various group combinations, the children will feel comfortable doing it for parents and special guests. Make sure that no children are coerced into performing if they do not want to. Be prepared to make last minute changes if necessary. A dancer could become a percussionist, for instance. Make sure the dancers and accompanists can concentrate on each other instead of on the audience. Otherwise, the performance will become an awkward recital instead of a showing and sharing of class work.

3

Skill-Development Movement Activities and Games

These skill-development movement activities are preliminaries to the improvisation machines (chapter 4) and include two categories: warm-up and isolation activities, and locomotor and axial movement games. Each category is designed to provide practice of movements the children already know and to promote the development of new skills. The movements discovered during these beginning sections of the movement session can be used in a more expressive way during the problem-solving phase of an improvisation machine later in the session. For example, you may remind the children that they may use the new skills they learned during a locomotor or axial movement game in their improvisation machines.

Warm-Up and Isolation Activities

The warm-ups are designed to build strength, endurance, and flexibility, and to develop spatial awareness. Isolation activities are designed to develop body awareness within the individual. Use warm-up and isolation activities to initiate participation and to bring the group together, as well as to get the blood circulating and the muscles stretched before the more rigorous locomotor and axial movement games to come.

When dancers and athletes warm up, it means exactly that, to warm the body by increasing the blood flow. Swings, gentle jogging, or sliding in a circle are quick and fun ways to get the heart pumping without putting stress on sensitive joints and muscles of the knees and ankles. Movements like jumping and leaping should be saved until the body has carefully warmed up, especially if your floor is cement or tile.

Warm-Up Activity 1: Swing-Swing-Circle-Swing

ACCOMPANIMENT: Music in threes with a moderate tempo or drumbeat.

DIRECTIONS: A swing is the bottom half of a circular movement with a drop-lift-drop-lift pendular quality. (Swings warm the body up by getting the heart pumping and by gently stretching the back, arm, neck, and leg muscles. If time is short, this could be your only warm-up.) Ask the group to form a large circle. Begin a swing of the torso, arms, head, and neck from side to side with the beat of the music, allowing the knees to soften on the drop and the arms and sternum to reach on the lift. You are now swinging from side to side in a vertical plane, keeping the movement in front of the body. Now begin a repetitive pattern of swing-swing-circle swing. To form the top half of the circle, simply continue moving the arms and torso in an arc and reach to the sky. Move to the beat of the music: swing (1-2-3), swing (2-2-3), circle (3-2-3), swing (4-2-3).

VARIATION 1: Travel around the circle by adding a slide step during the circle measure. You may want to circle only the arms as the slide occurs.

VARIATION 2: Add a full turn instead of circling the torso. If children have trouble getting all the way around, ask them to point to something or someone directly in front of them. Then say, "Can you point only with your eyes? This is called focus, and it will help you turn. See if you can look at that thing, or person, as soon as possible when you turn." Now the pattern is swing-2-3, swing-2-3, look-turn-look, swing-2-3.

Warm-Up Activity 2: Stretching

ACCOMPANIMENT: Music.
DIRECTIONS: There are two types of stretches, ballistic and static. The former, which is not recommended, is done with a gentle pulse or bounce and gives a short-term effect. For a more lasting stretch in a muscle, let gravity and body weight do all the work. Hanging, breathing, and relaxing during a stretch will give more lasting results.

Warm-Up Activity 3: Reach-Twist-Curl-Uncurl

ACCOMPANIMENT: Music with a regular rhythm and tempo.
DIRECTIONS: Begin with a reach to the sky. The movement begins in the legs and moves through the spine, out the crown of the head, and through dropped shoulders into the arms. Twist to the back and see what is behind you. Then curl down through each vertebra. Start with the head and neck, letting the weight of the head, neck, and arms slowly curl you down the spine. Feel the space between each vertebra lengthen. Do not bounce; just hang. You may keep your legs straight, or you may soften your knees if your legs are not stretched enough. Then uncurl the spine, vertebra by vertebra, to resume a standing position. You should feel much taller and stronger. Do one of the four movements with each measure of the music. If your music is in 4/4 time, the pattern will be reach (1-2-3-4), twist (2-2-3-4), curl (3-2-3-4), uncurl (4-2-3-4).

Warm-Up Activity 4: Yoga Shapes

ACCOMPANIMENT: Drum.

DIRECTIONS: Yoga shapes are a wonderful way to stretch. Use Rachel Carr's *Be a Frog, a Bird, a Tree* as a guide to shapes. Choose three shapes that will stretch the body on different levels. Choose the turtle, the bridge, and the tree, for example. Use the book's photos and short descriptions as instructions. Help the children who want help and tell the others who are having trouble doing the exact shape to invent their own turtle or their own balancing bird. Breathing is an important part of yoga, so ask the children to let the air in their lungs out slowly and to see if their shapes can keep growing, stretching, and reaching during the exhale. This can be a rather inactive activity for the children, so afterward play a game with the shapes. With the drum, indicate a running beat, then a freeze. Then call out a yoga shape. Use all three actions several times, varying the choice of locomotor steps. The last time say, "Do your favorite yoga shape."

Isolation Activity 1: Shakers

ACCOMPANIMENT: Tambourine or maracas.

DIRECTIONS: This activity aids in self-awareness by concentrating movement on only one part of the body at a time. Jiggle, wiggle, and shake each body part one at a time asking, "Can you move only one body part at a time? Move only your head to this beat, 1-2-3-4, and repeat. Now double-time, or twice as fast, 1 & 2 & 3 & 4 &. Repeat, and stop." Then ask, "What direction is your head pointing?" Say that your own head is pointing to the back, the side, or other appropriate direction. Repeat these questions with other body parts in isolation in sequence from head to toe, or from toe to head.

VARIATION 1: Change the tempo.

VARIATION 2: Emphasize the vibratory movement quality by asking

Yoga Shapes, a Warm-Up Activity

the children to make vibratory or sizzling sounds to go with the shaking movements.

Isolation Activity 2: Fantastic Elastic

ACCOMPANIMENT: Silence.

DIRECTIONS: Isolation means moving only one body part at a time. (This type of activity takes great concentration, and it exercises a child's sense of body awareness and spatial orientation.) Fantastic Elastic may be used as a stretching exercise or as an isolation activity. Give each child an imaginary piece of elastic. Ask, "How far can the elastic stretch? How long can it get before it snaps back? Now attach one end to your elbow and the other end to your knee. Stretch until it snaps back into place." Let the children think of the next body parts (arms and legs, toes and ears) to attach with the elastic. Ask the children to attach one end of the elastic to the floor and to stretch the other end toward the ceiling for one long, final stretch together.

VARIATION: Add music. Use a resonating instrument such as a triangle or gong for the stretching part. Try a sharp staccato instrument such as a drum or claves for the final snap-back part.

Isolation Activity 3: Addition and Subtraction

ACCOMPANIMENT: Classical guitar or piano. The solo instrument complements the isolated movement of body parts.

DIRECTIONS: Begin movement in a small part of the body, such as fingers or toes. Add adjacent body parts one at a time until the total body is involved. Then subtract body parts by freezing them one at a time until only one small part is left moving. This kind of isolation exercise takes concentration and repetition, but it is fun.

Locomotor and Axial Movement Games

In addition to the four dance elements, it is important that you know both the locomotor and the axial movement possibilities. Locomotor movements travel through space and involve a transfer of weight from one body part to another. Some examples of locomotor movements are: walk, run, jump, hop, leap, gallop, slide, skip, prance, crawl, somersault, and cartwheel. Axial movements are those occurring on a stationary base around the body's own vertical plane. Axial movements include swinging, twisting, bending, stretching or reaching, pushing, pulling, and rising and sinking.

Locomotor movements are those used to change location or to travel across the floor. All locomotor movements can be performed in any direction: forward, backward, sideward, or on the diagonal. When the group performs these movements together, remind the children to move to the empty spaces. The following basic locomo-

25

Prancing, a Locomotor Movement

tor movements may be alternated during any of the locomotor games.

> The *walk* is the simplest and most natural form of locomotion. The heel touches the floor first, and a transfer of weight takes place from one foot to the other in an even rhythm. Observe the tempo of the children's walk and adjust your drumming.
>
> The *run* also has an even rhythm and a transfer of weight from one foot to the other. The run is faster and requires more energy than the walk, and the run requires a push off the floor.
>
> The *jump* is a springing movement that lifts the body into the air. The takeoff can be from either one or both feet, but the landing should always be made with both feet simultaneously. Very young children may have trouble taking off from one foot and landing on two feet. Suggest that these children use both feet for takeoffs and landings. Suggest that the children push the floor away with their toes and that they land with no sound

Leaping, a Locomotor Movement

on the floor. Ask the children to make soft landings by bending their knees and ankles. The children will delight in the height of their jumps. Their legs may be open, closed, bent, or straight while they are in the air.

The *hop* is a jump on one foot. Both the takeoff and the landing are made with the same foot. The knees should bend upon landing. Be sure to give each foot equal time. For example, do eight hops on the right foot and eight hops on the left foot. If done this way, the hop is a precursor to the skip, which alternates legs with each step.

The *leap* is a pushing-off movement into the air that requires a transfer of weight from one foot to the other. During the period between the takeoff and the landing, the body is suspended in the air and both feet are off the floor. Describe a leap to the children as a giant step that goes into the air. Leaping over soft objects such as scarves or beanbags (one soft object at a time for two- and three-year-olds or several soft objects in a series for four- and five-year-olds) may improve the children's leaps.

The *gallop* is a combination of a step and a leap. One foot always maintains a lead. The gallop has an uneven rhythm and two weight transfers. The gallop's rhythm is long, short-long, short, long-short. Ask the children to chant the word gallop as they

27

move. The uneven rhythm is inherently in the word. The knees are raised slightly for a low gallop and to waist level for a high gallop. The higher gallop will naturally travel at a slower tempo.

The *slide* is a combination of a step and a run. The lead foot slides along the floor to an open position and the knees bend. The legs are then quickly pulled together as the free foot replaces the lead foot. The slide is often done in a sideways direction. The slide has an uneven rhythm and two weight transfers. The slide's rhythm is step-close-step, step-close-step.

The *skip* is a combination of a step and a hop that alternates from one foot to the other (step-hop, step-hop). Emphasis may be on height, quickness, or lightness.

The *roll* is a movement that travels by transferring weight to adjacent body parts after an initial impulse. Somersaults, log rolls, and rocks are examples of rolls.

Locomotor Movement Game 1: Stop and Go

ACCOMPANIMENT: Drum.
DIRECTIONS: The drum is your signal for Stop and Go. The children travel to the given rhythmic beat. They freeze when the drum stops. Accent the last drumbeat to emphasize the freezing. Vary the locomotor movements and challenge the children to stop in shapes they have never made before. Point out the different levels of the children's shapes and suggest twisted, wide, or tall shapes. Tell the group that you are going to touch the shapes that are still and strong. Suggested locomotor movements are: walk, run, gallop, skip, or slide. Small bouncing jumps are similar to the run, and higher jumps are similar to the walk.
VARIATION 1 (PARTNERS): Give the children six drumbeats to find a friend to move with. Tell them that they are going to stay together by looking at each other's eyes instead of by holding hands. Tell them that this is called focus. Take a minute to discuss the different

Stop and Go, a Locomotor Movement Game

eye colors in the group. Suggest that focusing on each other's eyes will work like magic in the partner game. Ask the partners to freeze in the same shape when the drum stops.

VARIATION 2 (SCULPTURE GARDEN): When the children freeze in their shapes, tell them that you are going to take a walk through their sculpture garden. Tell them that you want the shapes to be ones you have never seen before and that the shapes need to look interesting from all sides. As you stroll between the sculptures, look at them from several angles and point out the various levels, as well as the curved and the straight lines in the designs. Point out that the negative spaces are part of the sculptures' designs. The children will quickly learn that the empty spaces, as well as their bodies, make up the whole design. As an alternative, take one child at a time with you to view the sculptures in the garden. As you walk and comment on each design, the observing child learns a great deal about the levels, the lines, and the stillness involved in

29

forming the shapes. The children seem to create their most unusual designs for their friends.

VARIATION 3 (TRAFFIC COP): This variation calls for hand signals to be given by a leader (first the teacher) who stands in the center of the room. Gestures, such as beckoning for forward, wrist circles for around, and hitchhiker-type motions for backwards, are agreed upon and practiced before the game begins. The idea is to follow the hand signals accurately while keeping the locomotor beat.

Locomotor Movement Game 2: Beanbag Leaps

ACCOMPANIMENT: Percussion instrument and lively, rhythmic music.

DIRECTIONS: Put a beanbag in the center of room and let each child, individually, run to and leap over the beanbag. Touch the children on the heads or call their names to let them know when it is their turn. Going over the object naturally takes a leap (a transfer of weight from one foot to the other) instead of a jump. If some of the children jump over the beanbag instead of leaping, explain that a leap is a giant step in the air. Use a percussion instrument to strike the beat just before the leap to help the child off the floor. After the beanbag game has been accomplished by most children (three-year-olds may have trouble tracking the beanbag with their eyes and leaping at the same time, but they still enjoy the game very much), find some very lively, rhythmic music for leaping and set five or six beanbags in a floor pattern. Suggested patterns for beanbags are: diagonal, circular, serpentine, and zigzag.

VARIATION 1: Ask the children to make a loud sound or to shout their names as they leap over the beanbags.

VARIATION 2: Ask the children to leap higher. Say, "To leap even higher, find a way to let your arms help." The children may open their arms or circle their arms to help them leap higher.

VARIATION 3: Ask the children to leap, to circle their arms, and to shout a sound at the same time. The children will find it exhilarating to use breath and movement together. Their movements will look more free and have more height and control.

VARIATION 4: Have partners leap over the beanbags together. Challenge the partners to go up at the same time. Adjust the distance of the beanbags so that the children alternate legs. Add an image of leaping animals and animal sounds. Ask the children what animals leap and you will have leaping leopards, lions, deer, and tigers. Keep the focus on the leap, using the image only as additional motivation.

VARIATION 5: When the children have had experience leaping, ask them to add a turn in the air to their leaps. In ballet this is called a tour jeté. Using their arms, the children are able to leap higher. The higher leap gives each child enough time in the air for the turn. This is a difficult skill, so only the children who feel confident should try this variation. Let them decide. The turns may be done either to the left or to the right. The children who can do this variation have mastered a difficult technical skill.

Locomotor Movement Game 3: Sticky

ACCOMPANIMENT: Drum.

DIRECTIONS: Sticky is similar to Stop and Go in that you alternate locomotor rhythms and accent the last beat. But this time you call out, "Sticky arms," and the children freeze in groups of two or more with their arms touching. Repeat using legs or knees or backs or some other body part. At first the sticky shapes might take place only on a standing level. Give the sculptures five drumbeats to change levels. Each time you call out "Sticky," the children's groupings will change. The last time ask the whole group to make one giant sticky sculpture.

Locomotor Movement Game 4: Here to There

ACCOMPANIMENT: Percussion instrument.

DIRECTIONS: Here to There is a follow-the-leader game in which the first child chooses a way to travel from here (where the group is) to there (across the room). You may put colored tape on the floor to mark the pathway. As the group watches the movement, ask them to describe it in terms of quality, shape, level, direction, and speed. For example, the child may travel smoothly in a crouched shape at a low level in a forward direction at a moderate speed. The children may notice some of these points before the first child is finished. When the first child is there, ask him or her to call another child to follow until all the children have crossed the room. The game is repeated until each child has a turn and a great variety of locomotor movements have been tried.

VARIATION 1: Ask, "Can anyone do the movement in double-time? Now can you repeat the movement in slow motion? Backwards?"

VARIATION 2: Add a quality tool. If the movement is a jump, ask the children how they can jump. Each child may jump in a different way. Suggest that the children jump like a bouncing ball or like an athlete (a pole-vaulter), or that they jump as if someone were chasing them. You may suggest that they jump and turn, or jump and clap. Or suggest that they do a silly jump, a monster jump, a crooked jump, or an angry jump.

Locomotor Movement Game 5: Pathways

ACCOMPANIMENT: Music or drumbeats.

DIRECTIONS: Using colored masking tape, mark three different patterns on the floor at one time. Try the following floor patterns.

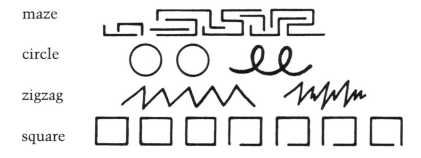

maze

circle

zigzag

square

triangle

spiral

open irregular curve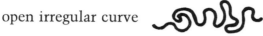

Have the children gallop, skip, run, tiptoe, and jump along the pathways. Then have the children change their direction of travel from forward to sideways and backwards.

VARIATION: Draw the floor pattern designs on cards and ask the children to travel with a chosen locomotor movement in a similar floor pattern. Ask them first to do the floor pattern in a small space and then to use the entire room.

Locomotor Movement Game 6: Rhythm

ACCOMPANIMENT: Drum.

DIRECTIONS: Choose three locomotor movements with different rhythms such as walk, run, and gallop. Divide the children into three or four groups, and assign each group one movement and a particular place in the room to start (such as the corners). The children should move all around the room to the appropriate rhythm and hurry back to the corner as soon as the rhythm changes and the next group begins to move. After each group has done all three basic movements, add a fourth locomotor movement that has a different rhythm, such as a giant step or a jump. To practice rhythmic responses for the first time, listen to the beat played on the drum. Then clap to the beat of the drum. Then add the locomotor movement to the clapping. The next step is to travel to the drumbeat without clapping. Here are the basic beats:

4/4 time (walk) 1 2 3 4

3/4 time (turn or spin) 1 2 3

2/4 time (slide or gallop) 1 & 2 &

4/4 time (run) 1 & 2 & 3 & 4 &

Locomotor Movement Game 7: Traveling Steps

ACCOMPANIMENT: Rhythmic accompaniment.
DIRECTIONS: Invite the children to do a traveling step that you call out (see locomotor movements). Then ask them to use variations such as adding arms, going to a higher or a lower level, changing direction or changing the step each time, and inventing a new locomotor step. Ask the children to remember all the traveling steps that you asked them to do and the ones that they invented. Point down a diagonal across the floor and ask the children to do a traveling step that will take them from here to there suddenly. Next ask the children if they can invent a traveling movement that will move them from here to there gradually. Divide the children into small groups of three or four. Ask them to do either the locomotor movements that moved them across the diagonal suddenly or those that moved them gradually.

Locomotor Movement Game 8: Movement Tag

ACCOMPANIMENT: Music that is appropriate for running or galloping, such as Latin and South American folk dance music.
DIRECTIONS: One child is "it." This child will choose a locomotor movement for the group to do such as the skip, the roll, the gallop, the walk, or the leap (see locomotor movements). Then the child who is "it" will chase the other children and will try to tag one of the children to be "it" next. The child who is "it" should do the same locomotor movement as the other children. When the next child is tagged, the children freeze to listen to the next chosen movement.

VARIATION 1: Ask the group to move backwards.

VARIATION 2: Try slow motion tag.

VARIATION 3: Try a game of circle tag. The children, except for two or more who are chosen to be "it," gallop, run, or jump in the form of a circle, while the children who are "it" move in the center of the circle. When the music stops, the children who are "it" must tag those children who are closest to them.

Locomotor Movement Game 9: Enter and Exit

ACCOMPANIMENT: Tape collage.

DIRECTIONS: This game combines Beanbag Leaps and Pathways with a polka dot segment. Beanbag Leaps, Pathways, and the polka dot segment are spatial awareness and locomotor activities that can be played separately or in combination for a new challenge. The children can help place colored dot stickers on the floor with enough space between the polka dots to dance between them. Place the colored tape (Pathways) in a simple maze or pattern on the floor and place the beanbags (Beanbag Leaps) in a circle on the floor. Instruct the children by saying, "When the music starts, do a traveling step to take you between the dots. When you get to the maze, tiptoe. When you get to the beanbags, leap over them. Finish by jumping up."

VARIATION 1: Have three small groups enter and exit from different directions.

VARIATION 2: Ask each group to enter and exit one at a time.

VARIATION 3: Have the children all go at once. Then ask the children to freeze when they hear their names. Then ask them to thaw when they hear their names again.

Axial movements occur on a stationary base. The body moves around its own vertical axis. In other words, the body does not travel in space. Some of the frequently used axial movements are defined below.

35

Stretching, an Axial Movement

Swinging is a release and a suspension in two even beats. The swing may be done with one isolated body part, such as the head or the arms, or with the torso, head, and arms upon bending knees.

Twisting is a rotation in two directions around the axis of the body. The twist is a spiraling movement that occurs mostly in the spine.

Bending is a movement starting in the spine that folds forward, arches backward, or moves sideward.

Stretching is a lengthening of the body or of body parts in any direction.

Pushing is a movement that exerts pressure away from the body in any direction in space.

Pulling is a movement that exerts pressure toward the body.

Swaying is a pendular, or back and forth, movement to a rhythm. Like a swing, a sway has a drop-lift-drop-lift effect, but the sway has a gentler motion than the swing.

Rising and sinking. Rising is a total body movement that gradually lifts one body part at a time off the floor. Its complement,

36

sinking, is a gradual release of energy from one body part at a time onto the floor.

Axial Movement Game 1: Balloons

ACCOMPANIMENT: Drumbeats or Paul Horn flute music.
DIRECTIONS: Ask the children to sink to the floor and to become flatter and flatter as they let the air out of their balloon shapes. Say, "Help me blow up the balloon in eight counts." With eight deep breaths, the balloon shapes will become taller, wider, and more round. Say, "Make sure that your balloon shape is curved and full of air but that it looks different than any other balloon shape." Then say, "Here comes a pin. Pop! Ssssss." Ask the children to take eight counts to let the air out. A popped balloon does not just sink like a rock to the floor, so encourage each balloon shape to show that sudden release of energy and perhaps to add a spin to the collapsing movement. Ask the children to hold the flattened, low-level, ending shape. With each repetition of this game, reduce the breathing counts from eight to four, to two, and then to one.
VARIATION: The children can cooperate to make a single balloon shape that pops into many fragmented shapes before spinning to the floor.

Axial Movement Game 2: Living Playground

ACCOMPANIMENT: Tape collage.
DIRECTIONS: Choose several movements associated with a park or playground setting and tell the children that you want to create a living, moving playground dance. Swinging, spinning, swaying, and bouncing movements are good starters because they are easily associated with playground swings, merry-go-rounds, trees, and see-saws, and also because they can be performed at various tempos and levels and as both solo and partner motions. Ask the children

not to begin their movements until the music starts. Say, "Beginning shapes ready?" before the music starts, and say, "When the music stops, hold your stillness." The children may either do only one playground movement or do all four before the music stops.

Axial Movement Game 3: Cloud Drifts

ACCOMPANIMENT: Gong, triangle, or bell.
DIRECTIONS: Either you or one of the children will play a gong, a triangle, or a bell. Ask four or five children to make a cloud shape. Explain that the cloud is to slowly and smoothly change shape with each beat and that the cloud is to hold a still shape when no sound is left. The cloud shape will continue to change as long as the resonating sound can be heard. If there is no sound, there is no movement. When the instrument is struck again, the cloud will again change shape. The change itself is more important than the resulting shape. A cause and effect relationship is established between percussionist and dancers. Dancers may take a turn with the gong or triangle or bell so that the cause and effect situation reverses periodically. This game is more effective with a group that has played the Sculpture Garden variation of Stop and Go, the locomotor movement game.

Axial Movement Game 4: Balances

ACCOMPANIMENT: Drum.
DIRECTIONS: Ask the children to find a new balance each time you hit the drum. You may get the children started by suggesting that they balance on one hand and one foot, or that they balance their weight on one hip. Or suggest that they find ways to balance on the small parts of their bodies. Ask the children to remember the best balances and to use them later in an improvisation machine (chapter 4).

4

Improvisation Machines

"A young child needs the security of a structure, a boundary, a cradle, a crib, a home, within which he/she can freely s-t-r-e-t-c-h."[7] An inexperienced but well-meaning teacher of children's dance once walked into the studio, put on a record, and said to a group of four-year-olds, "Now do whatever you want." Three children played ring around the record player, two headed right for the piano, and one opened his lunch. There was a lot of movement, but there was no form, no artistic expression, and definitely no dance.

Creative movement can be free only if it exists within the bounds of an improvisation machine. Improvisation machines are structured dance activities that have many possible movement solutions, and they are the core of the creative movement experience. A machine has form and function, and its confines define what is allowed and what is not allowed. Movement gains purpose and form within the boundaries of an improvisation machine. Form is "the organization of motor elements into a meaningful, visible pattern."[8]

Improvisation is spontaneous and requires no demonstration.

7. Anne Leif Berlin, *Teaching Your Wings to Fly. The Non-Specialists Guide to Movement Activities for Young Children* (Santa Monica, Calif.: Goodyear Publishing Co., 1971), vii.
8. Margaret N. H'Doubler, *Dance—As Creative Art Experience* (Madison: University of Wisconsin Press, 1968), 133.

Each practice session is different and each performance is new. However, improvisation improves with practice. Improvisation machines that work well once may work better the next time because expanding the children's movement repertoires takes time. And as more movement options become available, the children's improvisations improve. As the improvisation machines are invented, repeated, and expanded, relationships with others in the group grow, observations with an eye for aesthetics are cultivated, and creative responses deepen. Improvisation machines allow the children to shine as individuals and to freely express themselves. Performing spontaneously also stimulates the children's ability to discern expressive movement in others' actions.

After you have tried several of the following improvisation machines with the children, you will surely want to create your own. Improvisation machines use the children's growing movement repertoires of locomotor and axial movements. Studio tested improvisation machines, some with props, some with music, some with words, all use the children's growing movement repertoires of locomotor and axial movements, and they all are based on the elements of dance. So to create an improvisation machine, first choose one of the four elements of dance (body, space, time, or quality), and then choose one or more specific tools from within that element (chapter 2). Tools from the body element include the total body and isolated body parts. Tools from the space element are size, shape, focus, direction, and level. Tools from the time element are rhythm, duration, and tempo. Tools from the quality element are sustained, swinging, percussive, suspended, vibratory, and collapse.

Next, select an image and an accompaniment that will be used. Music, sound effects, or body music (clapping or stomping) can often provide an image. Imagery can also come from words, songs, stories, photographs, props, the environment, or activities in the children's lives. Give short, concise directions or titles for the improvisation machines.

Give the children time, about five to ten minutes, to explore movement solutions for each improvisation machine. It takes time to develop nonverbal communication channels. Remind the children of the locomotor and axial movements that they discovered during the warm-up and isolation activities and the movement games. Then the improvisation machines will be ready to be shared, either as solos, duets, or by half the class at a time. Ask the children who are waiting for their turns to watch for the elements and images in their friends' work. The children will clap and watch actively. Soon they will notice and recognize the elements of dance as they occur. Since each improvisation machine will be quite short, probably under one minute, the children in the audience are not asked to wait long for their turns to dance. The improvisation machines that follow are based on the above guidelines.

Improvisation Machine 1: Movement Sequence

ELEMENT: Space.
TOOLS: Direction and level.
IMAGE: Movement words.
ACCOMPANIMENT: Contrasting movement words used in a sequence and percussion instruments.
DIRECTIONS: The whole group may move into the empty spaces, or the children may move one at a time. Begin with a movement-word sequence such as gallop, gallop, gallop, balance, collapse, roll. Add the percussion accompaniment and ask the children to move as you say each word. Encourage level changes. You may suggest low-level movements such as crawling or rolling, or high-level movements such as jumping. Repeat each sentence three or four times. Half the group at a time may show this improvisation. The children will begin to help create the movement sequences after doing a few offered examples. Three suggested movement sequences follow.

Tiptoe, tiptoe, tiptoe, halt,
tiptoe, tiptoe, tiptoe, halt,
duck, crawl.

Movement Sequence, an Improvisation Machine

Run, run, run, jump, spin,
three giant steps in different directions,
stretch, bend, push, pull.
Run, run, run, leap, collapse, stretch,
spin, spin, spin, bend, push.

Improvisation Machine 2: Pulse

ELEMENT: Time.
TOOLS: Rhythm and tempo.
IMAGE: Heartbeat.
ACCOMPANIMENT: Heartbeat or pulses.
DIRECTIONS: The whole group will move together. Help the children find their pulses. Suggest that each child rest three fingers just under the thumb on the wrist of the opposite hand. Ask the children to be silent so that they can feel their pulses. Next ask them to

show the rhythm of their pulses by tapping their feet. Then ask them to use another movement and a different body part to indicate the same rhythm. Next ask the children to walk around the room. Then ask them to check their pulses again. Ask them to invent a movement that is the same tempo. Of course, as the children move, their pulse rates will increase. So the next movements that they invent will be faster. For example, they may run or gallop. Continue to stop, to check pulses, and to discover movements with the same tempo. When the pace has accelerated to a frenzy, suddenly ask the group to collapse on the floor. Ask that they cover their hearts with their hands and that they remain still until their heartbeats return to normal. Then ask them to sit up and get ready to try again.

Improvisation Machine 3: Percussion Games

ELEMENT: Quality.
TOOLS: Sustained, percussive, and vibratory.
IMAGE: Instruments and their sounds.
ACCOMPANIMENT AND DIRECTIONS: Ask the children to make beginning shapes in the empty spaces, where they will wait and listen for musical cues. Challenge the children to respond to each percussive sound with the appropriate movement quality tool. Remind them to hold still shapes until each new sound is heard. Have the children practice matching the movement quality tools with the percussive sounds before the improvisation begins. For instance, a gong or a triangle corresponds to sustained movements, which have an even flow and no pauses or stops. Ask that the movements continue until the reverberation fades entirely. Claves or woodblocks correspond to percussive movements with sudden stops (move and stop). Maracas or other shakers correspond to vibratory movements (shake, shake, shake). The children will alternate the roles of musician and dancer.

43

Boats and Bridges, an Improvisation Machine

Improvisation Machine 4: Boats and Bridges

ELEMENT: Space.

TOOLS: Shape and direction.

IMAGE: Boats and bridges.

ACCOMPANIMENT: Music and drumbeats.

DIRECTIONS: Ask four or five children to make bridge shapes. Ask the children to make new bridge shapes with each drumbeat. Give them at least eight counts in between drumbeats. Each bridge must have enough empty space under it to accommodate a boat passing through. Ask two children at a time to move like boats. When the music begins, the boats travel under as many bridges as possible before the music ends. Tell the boats that their shapes must conform to the space under the bridges so that the bridges will not break as the boats pass through. If the bridge shapes get tired, ask them to lower themselves to the floor very slowly so that a boat does not get stuck.

Ribbon Dance, an Improvisation Machine

Improvisation Machine 5: Ribbon Dance

ELEMENTS: Body and space.

TOOLS: Total body, isolated body parts, and direction.

IMAGE: Ribbons.

ACCOMPANIMENT: Choose a very different piece of music each time this improvisation is repeated.

DIRECTIONS: Challenge the children to move with the music and to keep the ribbons and their bodies moving continuously until the music stops. The ending shape should incorporate the ribbon in its design.

VARIATION 1: Have each child use two ribbons, one in each hand.

VARIATION 2 (HOLIDAYS): For Christmas, use part of Tchaikovsky's "Nutcracker Suite" for an accompaniment, and use festive red, green, silver, or gold ribbons. For St. Patrick's Day, use Irish folk music and green ribbons. For Halloween, try some spooky sound effects and black ribbons.

Improvisation Machine 6: Pass the Drum

ELEMENT: Time.
TOOL: Rhythm.
IMAGE: Echo of rhythm patterns.
ACCOMPANIMENT: Rich-sounding slit drum, large tom-tom, or a small conga drum.
DIRECTIONS: Ask the children to form a circle. Ask the first child to go to the middle of the circle and to play a short rhythm pattern on the drum. Ask the second child to move through the middle of the circle to the drumbeat and to freeze in an ending shape when the drum stops. Then ask the children forming the circle to echo the drum by clapping the rhythm as accurately as possible. Ask the dancer and the drummer to listen and to watch so that they can stop together and hold their stillness until the echo response is completed. Then ask the children to chant, "Pass the drum, pass the drum, pass the drum, drum, drum." The drummer will rejoin the circle, the dancer will become the next drummer, and a new dancer will be chosen. The turns progress around the circle until everyone has been offered a chance to drum and to dance. If the circle group gets restless, ask them to rub their hands together to warm up for the next clapping echo.
VARIATION 1: Ask that the next rhythm patterns be at a very fast tempo or at a very slow tempo.
VARIATION 2: Ask the dancer to move more slowly or more quickly than the drummer's tempo.

Improvisation Machine 7: Mirrors

ELEMENT: Space.
TOOL: Level.
IMAGE: Mirrors and reflections.
ACCOMPANIMENT: Music or drum.
DIRECTIONS: Ask the children to take partners. One child will be

the body and the other will be the reflection. The movement begins in one body part such as the hands and progresses to the arms, the upper torso, and so forth. When concentration is at its peak, ask the pairs to do locomotor movements as they continue mirroring. Tell the body to do movements that the reflection can follow easily. Use appropriate music, such as free-form jazz, or use a drum to keep time. When the music stops, both the body and the reflection must freeze. Then ask the children to switch roles. This is a standard dance and theater improvisation that takes a great deal of concentration. When showing the mirror improvisation to the group, choose two or three duets to perform at once, reminding the performers to focus on each other.

VARIATION 1: Begin the mirroring with one body part, and progressively add other parts until the pair is doing full body movements. Then gradually eliminate the body parts, one at a time. For example, begin with the hands, and then add the arms, the head, and the upper torso. If concentration is good, add the spine, the legs, and a traveling movement. Then reverse the progression; eliminate the traveling movement, the legs, the spine, the upper torso, the head, the arms, and finally the hands. The whole study should last only forty-five to sixty seconds.

VARIATION 2 (SAME AND DIFFERENT): In this variation of Mirrors, two rhythm instruments are used as signals. The partners begin by assuming identical beginning shapes. When the drum starts, the reflection copies the initiator. The body and the reflection will be the same. But when the second instrument starts to play, the reflection is set free to move as desired. The body and the reflection's movements will be different. When the drum starts again, the reflection must once again copy the initiator. When the dancers become proficient, switch instruments more rapidly.

Improvisation Machine 8: Hand Dance

ELEMENTS: Body and space.
TOOLS: Isolated body parts and direction.

IMAGE: Hand movements.
ACCOMPANIMENT: Jazz music with percussive sounds.
DIRECTIONS: Ask the children how many ways their hands can move. In response, the children may show that their hands can wiggle, shake, hide, flex, point, say hello, stretch taffy, spread honey, squeeze mud, shake something off, and that their hands can pretend to talk to each other. Say, "When the music begins, show how many different ways your hands can move. Be sure to use the space above, behind, and beside you. Hold your stillness when the music stops."

Improvisation Machine 9: Paint the Space

ELEMENTS: Space and quality.
TOOLS: Direction, level, and various quality tools.
IMAGE: Paint and canvas.
ACCOMPANIMENT: Recorded percussion music.
DIRECTIONS: Ask the children to imagine a giant pot of paint in front of each of them. Tell them to keep the color in their pots a secret. Ask the children to dig their fingers, hands, and wrists into the pretend paint pots with a slow reaching gesture. Ask each child to hold a beginning shape with a handful of imaginary paint. When the music begins, ask the children to paint the space surrounding each of their bodies (above, below, and to all sides) with hand, finger, and wrist movements. Since the music will have a variety of sounds, the resulting movement qualities will vary from delicate vibratory finger movements to strong, percussive hand gestures. Ask the children to hold their ending shapes when the music stops. You may allow the children to paint for thirty to forty seconds at a time.
VARIATION: Use the entire arm (up to the shoulder) to dip into the paint.

Improvisation Machine 10: Photo Images

ELEMENTS: Space, time, and quality.
TOOLS: The children will use those that fit the visual image.
IMAGE: Photos.
ACCOMPANIMENT: Silence.
DIRECTIONS: Give each child a picture, which is similar to that of a shooting star, a waterfall, sand dunes, fireworks, melting ice, or an erupting volcano (check *Time-Life* and *National Geographic* books for lovely photos). Challenge the children to use movements that describe the size, shape, direction, speed, and force of the images as they act them out. One child will act out a photo image. When finished, this child will hold an ending shape. At this time, the other children will guess what the image is. Explain that if the image is guessed right away, it was a good descriptive movement study. The children can take turns acting out their images.
VARIATION 1: Small groups of five or six children can move together to act out the same image and end in a group shape.
VARIATION 2: Ask each group or individual to add sound to the image study.

Improvisation Machine 11: Sixteen-Second Dance

ELEMENT: Time.
TOOL: Duration.
IMAGE: Ask the children to say how this movement makes them feel and you will have a variety of images.
ACCOMPANIMENT: Music or drum.
DIRECTIONS: You may use sixteen drumbeats or sixteen seconds of music, or you may use a stop watch to time exactly sixteen seconds. Tell the children when to go and when to freeze as you give them the following three instructions. "Please do as many movements as you can in sixteen seconds." "Now try only one movement that takes sixteen seconds to complete. That felt very different and it

looked like you had a lot of control." "Now try traveling away from your spot and back in sixteen seconds. That was tricky. Some dancers traveled away quickly and back slowly, while some traveled away slowly and made it back in two quick jumps. Try it again. This time try a way you have never tried before."

VARIATION: Combine the three sixteen-second segments above to create a dance with three sixteen-second sections. Say, "Go," to begin, and to halt the motion say, "Find an ending shape and hold your stillness."

Improvisation Machine 12: Onto the Mat

ELEMENT: Space.
TOOL: Direction.
IMAGE: Tumbling mat, which serves an imaginary river or ocean.
ACCOMPANIMENT: Have the children play percussion instruments.
DIRECTIONS: Place a tumbling mat near the end of the room's diagonal. Ask the children to imagine that the floor is the bank and that the mat is the river, or that the floor is the beach and that the mat is the ocean. Ask them to find new ways to travel on each surface. Ask the children to invent a special movement for traveling to the mat and to suddenly change the movement when on the mat. Ask the children to make the change sudden and exciting. Have the children play percussion instruments for the accompaniment.

Improvisation Machine 13: Words

ELEMENTS: Space and quality.
TOOLS: Shape, and quality tools that match the word image.
IMAGE: Words.
ACCOMPANIMENT: Vocal sounds.
DIRECTIONS: Say an emotion word such as "excited" or "shy," and ask one child to make a shape and a sound to go with it. Touch the

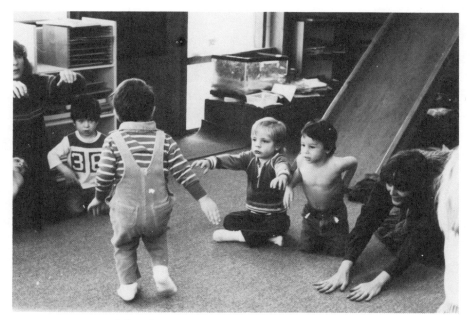

Words, an Improvisation Machine

child's head as a signal to begin. Next, ask one child for a word and ask another child to perform the word's image when touched on the head. The children's movements and sounds should answer the question, "What does it look like and how does it sound?" Encourage unusually shaped, unexpected movement responses and rhythmic vocal sounds. Your observations of the dance elements, including level, duration, shape, and direction, will encourage creative responses.

VARIATION: This word game can be played with emotion words or with other categories of words such as machines, animals, and natural events (waterfalls, comets, storms).

Improvisation Machine 14: Circus Train

ELEMENT: Space.
TOOL: Shape, level, size, and focus.

IMAGE: Circus train.

ACCOMPANIMENT: Circus music.

DIRECTIONS: Mark off a circus train on the floor with colored dot stickers. Ask each child to get on the train and to make the beginning shape of a circus performer or animal. Ask them to pay attention to shape, level, size, and focus. Tell a story along this theme.

> I'm a circus train driver, and since the circus is over, I must make sure that all performers are aboard this train so that we can take off. "All aboard! All aboard!" One little monkey escapes and unlocks the train cars and turns on the circus music and the circus begins again.

The performers and animals leave the train cars and move like their circus characters. Encourage lions and tigers to crawl on different levels, acrobats to change direction and speed, high wire walkers to walk on vertical or zigzag wires, giraffes to be long, smooth, and graceful, elephants to show every body part to be heavy and swinging, and encourage some clowns to move faster than the music, others slower. When the music stops, all performers and animals will sprint back to their spot on the train where they will make ending shapes.

VARIATION: The circus train could be a flower garden, a jungle, or a toy store. Or try using characters from a favorite story.

Improvisation Machine 15: Music, Music, Music

ELEMENT: Quality.

TOOLS: Quality tools are chosen to match musical images.

IMAGE: Contrasting musical images.

ACCOMPANIMENT: Tape collage with three contrasting musical selections or three pieces of unusual music or sound effects that the children have not heard before.

DIRECTIONS: Suggest that the children move as though the music is coming from within them. As each piece of music ends, ask the children to hold a pose until the next piece of music begins. Comment on the variety of shapes and movements that the children discover.

Improvisation Machine 16: As If

ELEMENTS: Time and quality.
TOOLS: Rhythm and various quality tools.
IMAGE: Sentences.
ACCOMPANIMENT: Silence.
DIRECTIONS: Ask the children to gallop as if the floor were made of deep mud, to slide as if the floor were made of cacti, to roll as if the floor were made of ice, and to jump as if the floor were made of soap bubbles. Divide the children into small groups and invent your own scenarios by choosing a movement and an "as if" for the floor. Let the children show the "as ifs" one group at a time. When the performing group has finished showing their study, the other children may guess what the movement and the "as ifs" were. The dance is not disturbed when the guesses are saved for the end.

Improvisation Machine 17: Turn the Corner

ELEMENTS: Time and space.
TOOLS: Rhythm, tempo, direction, and level.
IMAGE: Musical changes.
ACCOMPANIMENT: A musical piece with frequent changes in rhythm, tempo, or pitch.
DIRECTIONS: Instruct the children to choose a locomotor movement and to change direction sharply each time the music changes. At first, reinforce changes in the music by calling out, "Turn the corner," with each musical change. Then ask the children to change levels each time the music changes. With practice, the movement

changes will automatically occur with the musical cues. Use the same piece of music a number of times so that the musical changes become familiar.

Improvisation Machine 18: Slow-Medium-Fast

ELEMENT: Time.
TOOL: Tempo.
IMAGE: Contrast in the music's tempo.
ACCOMPANIMENT: A drum and music with a moderate tempo and an even rhythm.
DIRECTIONS: Divide the class into three small groups. All three groups will start with the music. The first group will move with the music at a medium tempo without traveling. The second group will move at a tempo much slower than the music without travel-ing. And the third group will move at a tempo much faster than the music. Ask the children to switch groups when the music stops. You may use one final count (played on the drum) to signal the switch.
VARIATION: Challenge the three groups to travel through the space together, remembering their tempos.

Improvisation Machine 19: Walk-Run-Collapse

ELEMENTS: Space and time.
TOOL: Direction and rhythm.
IMAGE: Contrast in speed.
ACCOMPANIMENT: Music that is the tempo of a walk.
DIRECTIONS: Divide the class into three small groups or simply let the children go three at a time. All three groups, or children, will start with music. Ask everyone to clap the beat of a walk, then the beat of a fast run, and finally to clap two beats as you say the word "collapse." One group, or one child, will walk all over the room,

the second will run in place as fast as possible, and the third will collapse in two counts into a shape on the floor. The challenge for those who walk is to cover as much space as possible, the challenge for those who run is to move as fast as possible, and the challenge for those who collapse is to hold the still shape until the music stops.

Improvisation Machine 20: Obstacle Course

ELEMENT: Space.
TOOL: Direction (over, around, under, across, through).
IMAGE: Props and direction words.
ACCOMPANIMENT: Direction words.
DIRECTIONS: Divide the group in half. One-half will leave the room for a few minutes. They may sing or tell a short story to keep busy. Challenge the other group to create an obstacle course on the floor, using any appropriate piece of school equipment (chairs, large blocks, parachutes, hoops, ramps, balance beams, very large balls, small trampolines, tunnels). Ask the children to keep the direction words in mind when they create the obstacle course. Call the others back into the room when the course is completed. The children in the group that created the course will give the directions to the others before they move through the course. For example, they may instruct the group to go around the rectangle blocks, slide across the ramp, jump over the cylinders, and crawl under the parachute. When this is accomplished, the groups switch roles; the second group will now build the new obstacle course. Make sure that the obstacle course is safe and that all equipment not being used is moved out of the way.

Improvisation Machine 21: Open and Shut Them

ELEMENT: Body.
TOOLS: Total body and isolated body parts.

Obstacle Course, an Improvisation Machine

IMAGE: The rhyme.
ACCOMPANIMENT: The rhyme.
DIRECTIONS: Open and Shut Them is a classic finger play rhyme used in many preschools and kindergartens. First, try the familiar rhyme with hand gestures.

> Open, shut them, open, shut them,
> Give a little clap, clap, clap.
> Open, shut them, open, shut them,
> Put them in your lap.
> Creep them, creep them, creep them, creep them,
> Right up to your chin.
> Open up your little mouth,
> But do not let them in!

To extend the range of movement possibilities, ask the children to open and shut isolated body parts, such as arms, legs, and hands, taking additional suggestions from the children.

VARIATION 1: Ask the children to open and shut their whole bodies to a musical accompaniment, freezing in an ending shape that is either very tightly closed or as open as it can be. Ask the children to find new open-and-shut movements that have not been tried before.

VARIATION 2: Ask the children to travel across the room one at a time in a very open shape. Ask them to open every part of their bodies, including their eyes, mouth, and fingers. Then ask the children to travel across the room in a very tightly closed shape. Say, "If your legs and feet are closed, how can you travel? Invent a new way to travel in a closed shape."

5

Session Endings

The session ending that you will use depends upon the children's concentration level, as well as how much time is left until the end of the session. Sometimes the children will need to relax. Other times they will be able to concentrate on choosing movements for a Good-Bye Dance. When emotions run in high gear, choose the Face Game to end the class. If the children still have a lot of energy, use Run-Jump-Catch. Try the following ways to end.

Session Ending 1: Rag Dolls

This ending is appropriate if the children need to relax. Sing or chant, "We are just rag dolls going limpidy limp, limpidy limpidy limp." Repeat this chant. Invite the children to imagine that they are becoming soft and limp and loose like rag dolls on a shelf. Circulate through the group lifting arms or legs to test how relaxed they are. Some children may need help to release enough muscle tension to be soft and loose. Lift these children slowly by both arms, checking to see that the head and neck relax. Assure these children that you intend to take gentle care of them and that you will let them back down softly. Ask each child to let go of more energy and to become more like a floppy rag doll.

Rag Dolls, a Session Ending

Session Ending 2: Run-Jump-Catch

Ask one child at a time to run toward you and jump into your arms. Use the child's weight and momentum to create a graceful swing before you put the child down in a different spot on the floor. The child's next jump may be higher. Finally, take a stationary pose. After a running start and a jump, each child will catch or attach to your body for a second. For just a moment the two of you become a group sculpture. Remind the children to wait for their name to be called or this improvisation could become run-jump-bump.

Session Ending 3: Good-Bye Dance

Use inspiring music that the children have not heard before. Ask the children to do a Good-Bye Dance, which may include move-

Run-Jump-Catch, a Session Ending

ments that they just did in previous sections of the movement session. Challenge the children to remember and perform as many movements as possible.

Session Ending 4: Face Game

Ask the children to cover their faces and to imagine what it feels like to get a surprise party. Then ask them to suddenly uncover their faces. Follow a similar procedure for other emotions, such as excitement, fright, anger, shyness, or sorrow, and observe the different facial expressions. To end the Face Game, you may extend the children's facial expressions to their feet by saying, "I see your excited faces. May I see an excited walk all the way to your shoes?"

Giant Yawn, a Session Ending

Session Ending 5: Giant Yawn

Play soft music. Ask the children to breathe deeply and to relax. Say, "Show me that you are tired by making a giant yawn with your whole body. Now stretch as wide as you can and make a yawning shape. Yawn to a friend. End with one last giant yawning shape that melts to the floor."

Session Ending 6: Hit the Tambourine

Have the children sit in a circle with red ribbons on their right hands and blue ribbons on their left hands. You will hold a tambourine in each hand. The tambourine in your right hand should have a red ribbon on it, and the one in your left, a blue ribbon. As you face each child, ask that child to strike the tambourine with the hand with the matching color. The children will be crossing the midlines

61

of their bodies and, thus, they will be improving their hand-eye coordination. The children will use both sides of the body without concern for the terms right and left.

Session Ending 7: Let's Race

Instruct the children by saying, "Let's race to your shoes. Start by all touching the wall. Ready. Set. Go to your shoes." When the children arrive at their shoes, call their names. For example, you may say, "Timmy won, and look who else won—Ellen, Jason, Molly," and so on, until each child's name has been called.

6

Sample Session

Preparation Activity 1: Shoe Train

ACCOMPANIMENT: Have music playing while the shoe train is forming so that the children can run or gallop to the music.
DIRECTIONS: Invite the children to make a long shoe train. Tell them that engines, tenders, boxcars, and cabooses are needed. Place your shoes against a wall and ask the children to add onto your engine. This game helps children who are reluctant to remove their shoes feel comfortable. Remember also to have the children remove their socks because socks are dangerously slippery on a wood floor and become loose and floppy during the vigorous leaping and jumping movements. Explain that dancers take good care of their bodies and that you do not want any slipping or tripping. Encourage the children to move together like a dance company, without bumping or falling, and to cooperate like a team.

Preparation Activity 2: A Beginning Circle

ACCOMPANIMENT: Music.
DIRECTIONS: The beginning of the session is a good time to work on

A Beginning Circle

cooperation, community effort, and the spatial awareness concept. Ask the children to form a circle. Say, "Come join us, we are starting all together." "Where can you put yourself to be a patch for our circle?" "Our circle has several empty spaces." "Where can you sit to help the circle become really round?" "Take good care of the circle."

Warm-Up or Isolation Activity

ACCOMPANIMENT: Drum or music.
DIRECTIONS: Ask the children to either sit or stand in a circle. Choose a warm-up or an isolation activity.

Locomotor or Axial Movement Game

ACCOMPANIMENT: Drum or other percussion instrument.
DIRECTIONS: Choose or invent a movement game using locomotor or axial movements that will extend the children's movement repertoires. Or work with an image taken from the children or the environment. The children may move together as a group into the

Open and Shut Them, an Improvisation Machine

empty spaces in the room, or they may move one at a time across the floor.

Improvisation Machine

ACCOMPANIMENT: The emphasis is on musical variety (folk, jazz, classical, sound effects). Tape collages are easily made with a cassette deck and a turntable or with two cassette decks. Tape collages allow more rapid changes in the music. Or you may have the children play percussive instruments for each other, trading the roles of musician and dancer.

DIRECTIONS: Choose, invent, or extend a dance improvisation (chapter 4). Concentrate on the elements of dance as you work. Each machine uses all four dance elements, but focusing on one or two at a time gives each improvisation its framework. Have half the group at a time show their improvisation machines, or have

65

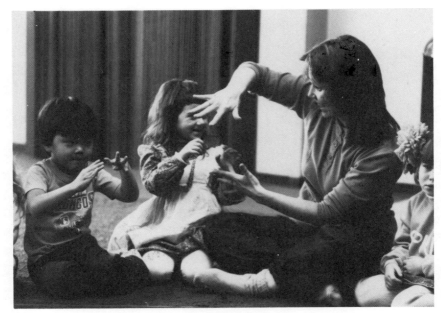

Hand Dance, an Improvisation Machine

small groups of two, three, or four children show their improvisations to the others. Some children may want to do solos. Alternate the roles of audience, sound person, and dancer. The sound person may operate the tape recorder or play the drum. Remind the children that the role of an audience is to watch quietly and to observe without putting a value judgment on the movement. In other words, ask the children not to laugh or chatter. Ask the children to clap at the end of each improvisation and to say thank-you. In this way, the group learns to see beauty in each dancer. It is helpful for preschoolers to have something to do while they watch and wait for a turn. Clapping, swaying, counting leaps, describing movements, and taking imaginary photos with pretend cameras are fun ways to wait.

VARIATION: As a transition, pretend to sell tickets to audience members. Show the children to their seats in the front row, asking them how much the tickets should cost and reminding them that they each will have a turn to perform. This variation may be done in the same manner as theater-in-the-round where all audience members sit in a large circle that defines a round stage area.

Ending

Choose either Rag Dolls, Run-Jump-Catch, Good-Bye Dance, Face Game, Giant Yawn, Hit the Tambourine, or Let's Race.

7

Children with Special Needs

Dr. A. Jean Ayres, an occupational therapist and the author of *Sensory Integration and the Child*, has defined sensory integration as the organization of sensation for use.[9] A child's central nervous system takes in and uses the sensations of touch, sight, smell, and hearing, and then puts them together in an adaptive response or in a useful motion.

Watching children move through space, teachers marvel at their smooth, beautiful movements and their seemingly effortless connection of their ideas and their motions. In order to complete these motor actions, the child's central nervous system does motor planning. Motor planning, or praxis, is to the physical world what speech is to the social world, according to Ayres. Motor planning involves arousal, ideation (concept formation), a plan for a course of action, and the execution of the plan. Children use their automatic ability to integrate sensations to perform desired actions. Ayres tells us that it is important for children to follow their inner drives to produce physical activity in which they master their bodies and their environment. Physical activity, such as creative movement, provides sensory stimulation that helps children organize their brains. Ayres stresses the importance of play, which provides oppor-

The illustrations in this chapter are solely for illustrative purposes and are not to suggest that the subjects in the photographs have experienced disabilities.

9. A. Jean Ayres, *Sensory Integration and the Child* (Los Angeles: Western Psychological Services, 1979), 5.

tunities for children to explore and to have their senses stimulated. Play contributes to children's development.[10] In creative movement, children are able to move their body parts in many ways. The sensations from these movements add new sensory input to the children's bodies. And children learn to relate to their surrounding space by using large, full body movements.

But children in your group who are not developing normally often need extra help to participate in activities such as creative movement. Many teachers wonder if it is possible to meet the needs of such children in a movement session. We have moved and danced with children experiencing disabilities ranging from mild to severe. These children were mainstreamed into regular preschool classes. We learned that parents and specialists who worked with these children were great sources of help in planning for the children's most successful participation. We learned more about these disabilities so that we could also teach the children better in other areas. These experiences helped us to personalize or individualize our teaching for all children. The teacher's challenge is to help each child use what he or she has.

Some children are uncomfortable with movement. They have the inner drive to produce physical activity, but they are not successful because they have a sensory processing disorder. Many of these children have not experienced how it feels to be centered in their own bodies or how it feels to be able to shift their weight. They may not be able to balance or to rotate from side to side. Thus, they may not be able to move rhythmically to music. Without normal movement experiences, related experiences of touch, sight, hearing, and rhythm are restricted. The combination of stability, or centeredness, and movement is the matrix within which the other sensations develop.[11] Visual direction may be hard for these children. You may remind them to look at what they are doing and where they are going. For example, in Here to There (chapter 3) or

10. A. Jean Ayres, *Developmental Dyspraxia* (Torrance, Calif.: Sensory Integration International, 1985), 1.

11. Lois Hickman, *Occupational Therapy: Sensory Integration International* (Longmont, Colo.: Expectations Unlimited, 1987), Audiotape.

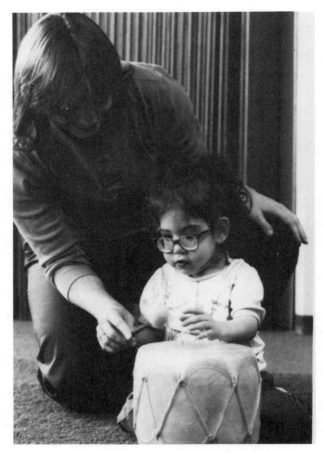

Teachers Personalize Their Teaching

in Enter and Exit (chapter 3), remind the children to focus on the tape or dots on the floor. Touching the body part that the child is going to use can direct vision to that part.

Children with sensory-processing disorders need the sensory input of creative movement, and they need to be accepted for their efforts. Helping these children express their inner drives by showing rather than telling accentuates what they can do rather than what they cannot do. Observe which movements are difficult for the child, and give the child support when needed. Respecting the

70

*Focusing on Tape
on the Floor Aids
Visual Direction*

child's need not to participate in some activities is also important. You may recommend that the parents get professional help for the child, and you may assist the parents in finding that help.

Remember that children who do not have use of their legs, as in the case of those with spina bifida or cerebral palsy, are able to experience visual and auditory stimulation, as well as upper body movement. Lois Hickman reminds us that the feeling of being grounded or centered must still be acknowledged. The fear that results from not having a sensation of balance or the freedom to move is a challenge for the children to overcome.

71

An Adult Can Be a Child's Legs

Work with the child's therapists and parents to help bridge the gap that has occurred due to the lack of normal developmental experiences.[12] A child who uses a wheelchair can experience the locomotor games alone or with help from another child. In addition, an adult can be this child's legs so that the child can experience what it is like to run across a large space (by being carried) and what it is like to stop in front of another person without bumping. Developing trust is an important part of working with children, especially when they are physically vulnerable. A young friend of Lois Hickman reminds us that the progression of activities needs to be "scary enough to be fun but not so scary that I won't try it."[13]

A child who cannot see can experience across the floor movements, such as Beanbag Leaps, by holding hands with a partner.

12. Hickman.
13. Hickman.

A Child May Provide a Musical Accompaniment

This partnership provides an opportunity for the child to develop trust, cooperation, and even a new friendship. Auditory experiences, including music and rhythm, enhance creative movement for this child.

Your ability to communicate is challenged when a child's hearing is impaired. You may learn new skills such as sign language to meet this child's needs. Good teaching also involves making the environment work for the learner, so visual cues and visual imagery will be important. Invite the child with a hearing loss to provide the music or drum accompaniment for any stop and go activity. This puts the child in control of the situation.

Children who are mentally retarded grow, learn, and experience joy through creative movement. Again, adapting to the strengths and needs of each child makes his or her experience successful. Music and rhythm are important to these children in ways that perhaps verbal imagery is not. Props, such as hats and scarves, promote participation. Explore clear, uncomplicated ways for the children who are retarded to follow directions.

Including children who are different in a creative movement class opens up new possibilities, ideas, cooperation, and learning for all who participate.

Assignments for Student Teachers

Bibliography

Assignments for Student Teachers

Chapter 1

1. Observe children in a school free play or playground setting. Jot down as many different movements as you notice for two children. Chart these movements, dividing them into two categories: mainly functional and mainly expressive. Discuss.

2. Select one visual and one auditory imagery idea that would appeal to the children. Discuss how you can use an image as a catalyst for movement ideas.

Chapter 2

1. Select a prop that can be manipulated easily by children. Use this prop and its physical properties, such as size, shape, weight, and color, as the basis for movement ideas.

2. Select a poem specifically for its movement word images. Ask the children to invent either shapes or movements for those words in the poem.

3. Observe ordinary movements from everyday life. Select one and

describe it in terms of the four dance elements and the specific tools within each element.

4. Plan an activity for a small space, a large space, and an outdoor space.

5. Prepare a movement activity using an object or an event that is familiar to children. Use an image that promotes total body involvement.

6. Use a children's book for movement activity ideas. Focus on character and plot as starters for movement sequences.

Chapter 3

1. Write and demonstrate both a locomotor and an axial movement game. Include floor patterns for the locomotor movement game, if applicable.

2. Prepare a warm-up activity that uses the whole body but that begins with one body part.

Chapter 4

1. Invent an improvisation machine. Be able to identify the elements of dance and the specific tools upon which the improvisation focuses. Include music.

Chapter 5

1. Invent a relaxation activity that may be used to end a movement session. Include music.

Chapter 6

1. Make your own sample session plan designed for your particular space, group size, and available time span.

Chapter 7

1. Create a movement activity specifically for children with sensory integration problems.

2. Discuss ways in which children with physical disabilities may be included in creative movement activities.

Bibliography

Ayres, A. Jean. *Developmental Dyspraxia*. Torrance, Calif.: Sensory International, 1985.

———. *Sensory Integration and the Child*. Los Angeles: Western Psychological Services, 1979.

Berlin, Anne Leif. *Teaching Your Wings to Fly: The Non-Specialists Guide to Movement Activities for Young Children*. Santa Monica, Calif.: Goodyear Publishing Co., 1971.

Berrol, Cynthia. "The Effects of Two Movement Therapy Approaches." *American Journal of Dance Therapy* 7 (1984): 32–48.

Canner, Norma. *And a Time to Dance*. Boston: Beacon Press, 1968.

Carr, Rachel. *Be a Frog, a Bird, a Tree*. New York: Doubleday and Co., 1973.

Graham, George. *Children Moving—A Reflective Approach to Physical Education*. Palo Alto, Calif.: Mayfield Publishing Co., 1980.

Hawkins, Alma M. *Creating through Dance*. Englewood Cliffs, N.J.: Prentice Hall, 1964.

H'Doubler, Margaret N. *Dance—As Creative Art Experience*. Madison: University of Wisconsin Press, 1968.

Hickman, Lois. *Occupational Therapy: Sensory Integration and Normal Development*. Longmont, Colo.: Expectations Unlimited, 1987. Audiotape.

Humphrey, Doris. *The Art of Making Dances*. New York: Gone Press, 1959.

Joyce, Mary. *First Steps in Teaching Creative Dance to Children*. Palo Alto, Calif.: Mayfield Publishing Co., 1979.

LaFond, Arisa. "Rainbows." *I Am Who I Am*. Boulder, Colo.: Boulder Children's Productions, 1985. Sound cassette.

Leboyer, Frederick. *Loving Hands*. New York: Alfred A. Knopf, 1976.

Lynch-Fraser, Diane. *Dance Play: Creative Movement for Very Young Children*. New York: Walker Publishing Co., 1982.

Murray, Ruth Lovell. *Dance in Elementary Education—A Program for Boys and Girls*. New York: Harper and Row, 1962.

Oppenheim, Joanne F. *Kids and Play*. New York: Ballantine Books, 1984.

Shawn, Ted. *Dance We Must*. New York: Haskell House Publishing, 1974.

Siegel, Marcia B. *Please Run on the Playground*. Hartford, Conn.: Connecticut Commission on the Arts, 1975.

———. *Watching the Dance Go By*. Boston: Houghton Mifflin Co., 1977.

Sullivan, Molly. *Feeling Strong, Feeling Free: Movement Exploration for Young Children*. Washington, D.C.: National Association for the Education of Young Children, 1982.

Ginger Zukowski began training at the University of Illinois, Champaign, in 1969 studying with Steve Paxton and Beverly Schmidt Blossom. She continued studies in dance education at Southern Illinois University and was a member of the Southern Illinois Repertory Dance Theater in 1972–73. Since moving to Colorado, Ginger has maintained her interest in modern dance and creative movement by teaching and studying at the Community Dance Collective, Community Schools, and the Colorado Dance Festival. She currently teaches at New Horizons Cooperative Preschool.

Ardie Dickson has been a teacher of young children and adults for the last twenty years. She is the director of and a teacher at New Horizons Cooperative Preschool, a non-profit multicultural parent cooperative school in Boulder, Colorado. Her bilingual children's book *Come to the Pond/Vengan al Estanque* was published in 1976. She is a graduate of University Without Walls at Loretto Heights College in Denver.